THE ADVENTURES OF
TOM SAWYER

Tom Sawyer likes adventures. When other people are sleeping in their beds, Tom Sawyer is climbing out of his bedroom window to meet his friends. He and Joe Harper and Huckleberry Finn have an exciting life. They look for ghosts, they dig for treasure, and they take a boat down the Mississippi to Jackson's Island—to swim, fish, and sleep under the stars.

But Tom's adventures can be dangerous, too. One night in the graveyard he and Huck Finn see three men. Who are they? And what are they doing in the graveyard, in the middle of the night? Then the boys see that one of the men is Injun Joe ...

Tom and Huck never forget that night. They are afraid of Injun Joe—and they are right to be afraid because Injun Joe is very quick with a knife ...

OXFORD BOOKWORMS LIBRARY
Classics

The Adventures of Tom Sawyer

Stage 1 (400 headwords)

Series Editor: Jennifer Bassett
Founder Editor: Tricia Hedge
Activities Editors: Jennifer Bassett and Alison Baxter

American Edition: Daphne Mackey, University of Washington

MARK TWAIN

The Adventures of
Tom Sawyer

Retold by
Nick Bullard

Illustrated by
Paul Fisher Johnson

OXFORD UNIVERSITY PRESS

OXFORD

UNIVERSITY PRESS

Great Clarendon Street, Oxford OX2 6DP

Oxford University Press is a department of the University of Oxford.
It furthers the University's objective of excellence in research, scholarship,
and education by publishing worldwide in

Oxford   New York

Auckland   Cape Town   Dar es Salaam   Hong Kong   Karachi
Kuala Lumpur   Madrid   Melbourne   Mexico City   Nairobi
New Delhi   Shanghai   Taipei   Toronto

With offices in

Argentina   Austria   Brazil   Chile   Czech Republic   France   Greece
Guatemala   Hungary   Italy   Japan   Poland   Portugal   Singapore
South Korea   Switzerland   Thailand   Turkey   Ukraine   Vietnam

OXFORD and OXFORD ENGLISH are registered trade marks of
Oxford University Press in the UK and in certain other countries

ISBN 978 0 19 423742 0

Printed in China

CONTENTS

1

Tom and His Friends

"Tom! *Tom*! Where are you?"

No answer.

"Where is that boy? When I find him, I'm going to …"

Aunt Polly looked under the bed. Then she opened the door and looked out into the garden.

"*Tom*!"

She heard something behind her. A small boy ran past, but Aunt Polly put out her hand and stopped him.

"Ah, there you are! And what's that in your pocket?"

"Nothing, Aunt Polly."

Aunt Polly put out her hand and stopped him.

1

"Nothing! It's an apple! I can see it. Now listen, Tom. Those apples are not for you, and I—"

"Oh, Aunt Polly! Quick—look behind you!"

So Aunt Polly looked, and Tom was out of the house in a second. She laughed quietly. "I never learn. I love that Tom, my dead sister's child, but he isn't an easy boy for an old lady. Well, it's Saturday tomorrow. There's no school, but it isn't going to be a holiday for Tom. Oh no! He's going to *work* tomorrow!"

Saturday was a beautiful day. It was summer, the sun was hot, and there were flowers in all the gardens. It was a day for everybody to be happy.

Tom was the unhappiest boy in the town.

Tom came out of his house with a brush and a big bucket of white paint in his hand. He looked at the fence; it was nine feet high and ninety feet long. He put his brush in the paint and painted some of the fence. He did it again. Then he stopped and looked at the fence, put down his brush, and sat down. There were hours of work in front of him, and he was the unhappiest boy in the town.

After ten minutes Tom had an idea, a wonderful idea. He took up the brush again and began work. He saw his friend Joe Harper in the street, but he didn't look at him. Joe had an apple in his hand. He came up to Tom and looked at the fence.

"I *am* sorry, Tom."

Tom said nothing. The paint brush moved up and down.

"I am *sorry, Tom,*" said Joe.

"Working for your aunt?" said Joe. "I'm going down to the river. I'm sorry you can't come with me."

Tom put down his brush. "You call this work?" he said.

"Painting a fence?" said Joe. "Of course it's work!"

"Maybe it is, and maybe it isn't. But I like it," said

Tom. "I can go to the river any day. I can't paint a fence very often."

Joe watched Tom for about five minutes. Tom painted very slowly and carefully. He often stopped, moved back from the fence, and looked at his work with a smile. Joe began to get very interested and said:

"Tom, can I paint a little?"

Tom thought for a second. "I'm sorry, Joe. You see, my aunt wants me to do it because I'm good at painting. My brother Sid wanted to paint, too, but she said no."

"Oh, please, Tom, just a little. I'm good at painting, too. Hey, do you want some of my apple?"

"No, Joe, I can't—"

"OK, you can have *all* my apple!"

Tom gave Joe the brush. He did not smile, but for the

Tom was the richest boy in St. Petersburg.

first time that day he was a very happy boy. He sat down and ate Joe's apple.

More friends came to laugh at Tom, but soon they all wanted to paint, too. By the afternoon Tom had three balls, an old knife, a cat with one eye, an old blue bottle, and a lot of other exciting things. He was the richest boy in St. Petersburg, and the fence—all ninety feet of it—was a beautiful white. He went back to the house.

"Aunt Polly! Can I go and play now?"

Aunt Polly came out of the house to look. When she saw the beautiful white fence, she was very pleased. She took Tom into the house and gave him an apple.

"Well, you can go and play. But don't come home late."

Tom quickly took a second apple and ran off.

On Monday morning Tom didn't want to go to school, but Aunt Polly got him out of bed, and then out of the house. In the street near the school he met his friend Huckleberry Finn. Huck had no mother, and his father drank whiskey all the time, so Huck lived in the streets. He didn't go to school, he was always dirty, and he never had a new shirt. But he was happy. The mothers of St. Petersburg didn't like Huck, but Tom and his friends did.

"Hello, Huck!" said Tom. "What do you have there?"

"A dead cat."

"What're you going to do with it?" asked Tom.

"I'm going to take it to the graveyard tonight," Huck said. "At midnight. A dead cat can call ghosts out of their graves."

"I never heard that," said Tom. "Is it true?"

"Well, I don't know," said Huck. "Old Mrs. Hopkins told me. Come with me and see. Or are you afraid of ghosts?"

"Of course not!" said Tom. "Come and meow for me at my window at eleven o'clock."

After this, Tom was late for school, and the teacher looked at him angrily.

"Thomas Sawyer, why are you late again?" he said.

Tom began to speak, and then stopped. There was a new girl in the schoolroom—a beautiful girl with blue eyes and long yellow hair. Tom looked and looked.

"A dead cat can call ghosts out of their graves."

Oh, how beautiful she was! And in two seconds Tom was in love! He *must* sit next to her. But how?

In the girls' half of the room there was only one empty chair, and it was next to the new girl. Tom thought quickly, and then looked at the teacher.

"I stopped to talk with Huckleberry Finn!" he said.

The teacher was very, very angry. Boys were often late for school. That was bad, but talking with Huckleberry

The teacher took his stick …

Finn was worse, much worse! The teacher took his stick, and two minutes later Tom's trousers were very hot, and the teacher's arm was very tired.

"Now, Tom Sawyer, you go and sit with the *girls*!"

Some of the children laughed. Tom walked to the chair next to the new girl, sat down, and opened his book. The other children began to work again.

After ten minutes, the girl looked up. There was an apple on the table in front of her. She put it back on Tom's half of the table. A minute later the apple was in front of her again. Now it stayed. Next, Tom drew a picture of a house and put it in front of her.

"That's nice," the girl said. "Now draw a man."

Tom drew a man next to the house. The man was taller than the house, and he had very big hands and very long legs. But the girl liked him.

8

"Can you draw me now?" she asked.

Tom drew a girl next to the man.

"You draw beautifully. I can't draw pictures."

"I can teach you," said Tom. "After school."

"Oh, please!"

"What's your name?" Tom asked.

"Becky. Becky Thatcher."

Just then Tom felt a hand on his head. It was the teacher. He took Tom by the ear and moved him back to his chair in the boys' half of the room.

"You draw beautifully," said the girl.

9

2

In the Graveyard

That night Tom went to bed at half past nine. He waited for Huck's meow, and at eleven o'clock it came. He climbed quietly out of the bedroom window, and then he and Huck walked out of the town with the dead cat.

The graveyard was on a hill, about a mile from St. Petersburg. When the boys got there, they put the dead cat on a grave and sat down behind some trees. They watched, and waited. It was very dark, and very quiet.

"Do you see that new grave there?" whispered Huck. "That's Hoss Williams' grave. He died last week."

"Perhaps he can hear us," Tom whispered back. "Do you think he can, Huck?"

"I don't know, but I—"

"*Sh*!"

"Oh, Tom, what is it?"

"*Sh*!" whispered Tom. "I can see something. Look!"

Huck moved nearer to Tom. "Ghosts!" he said. "Three of them! They're coming here, Tom! Oh, let's go home!"

"They can't see us," Tom whispered. "Not here."

"Ghosts can see through trees," said Huck unhappily. "They can see through everything!"

The ghosts moved quietly through the graveyard and

"They're not *ghosts."*

came nearer to the trees. Huck and Tom watched, very
afraid. Then, after a minute, Huck said:

"Tom! They're *not* ghosts. That's Muff Potter."

"So it is. And that's Injun Joe. And the other man is
Doctor Robinson. What are they doing here?"

"They're grave robbers, Tom! They're going to rob a
grave! My father told me about it. The doctor wants a

dead body, you see. He cuts it up because he wants to learn about—"

"Sh!" said Tom. "They're getting near."

Injun Joe and Muff Potter began to dig.

The three men stopped at Hoss Williams' grave, and Injun Joe and Muff Potter began to dig. Ten minutes later the grave was open.

"Now, doctor," said Muff Potter. "You want us to take the body to your house? That's five dollars more."

"No!" said the doctor. "I gave you the money this morning. I'm not giving you any more!"

"Now you listen to me, doctor!" said Injun Joe. "I want that money! Do you remember that day five years ago? I came to your house and asked for something to eat. And you gave me nothing. Nothing! So give me that money!"

He took the doctor's arm, but suddenly the doctor hit him, and Injun Joe fell to the ground.

"Don't hit my friend!" cried Muff Potter. He jumped on the doctor, and the two men began to fight.

It all happened very quickly, and the two boys watched with open mouths. Injun Joe got up. He had Muff Potter's knife in his hand now, and he moved behind the doctor. Then the doctor hit Muff Potter on the head. Muff fell to the ground, and at the same

Injun Joe moved behind the doctor.

moment the knife in Injun Joe's hand went into the doctor's back. The doctor fell to the ground, on top of Muff Potter, and he did not move again.

The two boys could watch no more. Very quietly, they moved away from the trees, and then ran out of the graveyard and back to the town.

Injun Joe stood by Hoss Williams' grave and looked down at the two men. Then he put the knife into Muff Potter's hand and sat down. Three—four—five minutes went by. Potter moved a little and opened his eyes.

"What—what happened, Joe?" he asked.

"This is bad, Muff," said Joe. "Why did you kill him?"

Muff looked at the doctor's dead body and then at the knife in his hand. "Me? Did I kill him?" His face went white, and the knife fell from his hand. "It's the whiskey, Joe! I never fight with knives usually. Oh, why did I drink all that whiskey tonight? I don't remember anything!"

"It's OK, Muff," said Joe. "I'm not going to tell anyone. You get away quickly. Go on—go now!"

Muff Potter got up and ran away. Joe watched him for a minute, then he carefully put the knife next to the doctor's body. Then he, too, left the graveyard.

—≪≪≪—

The next day the Sheriff's men found the doctor's body in the graveyard—and Muff Potter's knife. That night Muff came back to the graveyard to get his knife. But the

And there Muff waited for his trial.

Sheriff's men were there, and they took Muff to St. Petersburg's little jail. And there Muff sat for four weeks and waited for his trial.

―≪≪≪―

Tom and Huck could not forget that night in the graveyard. They were very unhappy, and very afraid.

"What're we going to do?" said Tom. "Muff Potter didn't kill the doctor—Injun Joe did. We *saw* him!"

"I know," Huck said. "But what *can* we do? We can't tell anyone. I'm afraid of Injun Joe. He's dangerous. And he's a killer. Do you want a knife in *your* back?"

"Yes, I'm afraid of him, too," Tom said. He thought for a minute. "I'm sorry for Muff Potter, but you're right, Huck. We can't tell anyone about Injun Joe."

3

On Jackson's Island

The summer holidays came, and there was no school.
Tom didn't want to think about Muff Potter and Injun
Joe, but it wasn't easy. At night, when he was in bed, he
saw Injun Joe's face in the dark, and he couldn't sleep.
But he couldn't talk to anyone about it.

One hot summer's day he and Joe Harper were down
by the Mississippi River. They sat and watched the
boats, fished, and talked.

"Let's get away from here!" said Tom, suddenly.
"Let's go and do something exciting somewhere."

"OK," said Joe. "But what? And where?"

"I know," Tom said. "Let's run away. Let's go and live

They watched the boats, fished, and talked.

on Jackson's Island. We can sleep out under the trees."

Jackson's Island was in the Mississippi, three miles south of St. Petersburg. Nobody lived there.

"Let's ask Huck Finn, too," said Tom. "But don't tell your mother or father or anyone. Go home and get some things to eat, and meet me here at midnight."

They cooked some of the meat over the fire.

So that night three boys in a small boat went down the river to Jackson's Island. They had some bread and some meat, and Huck had his pipe, too. When they got there, they carried everything on to the island and made a fire under a big old tree. Then they cooked some of the meat

The three boys ran down to the river to swim.

over the fire, and oh, that meat was good—the best dinner in the world! Soon, they stopped talking, their eyes closed, and they slept.

The next morning Tom woke up with the sun on his head and a smile on his face. Then Huck and Joe woke up, and the three boys ran down to the river to swim. After that, they fished, and soon they had about six big fish for their breakfast. They cooked the fish on their fire and ate them all. They were very hungry.

"That," said Joe happily, "was a wonderful breakfast!"

After breakfast they walked through the island, swam some more, talked, fished, and swam again. They came back to their fire in the afternoon. Suddenly, Tom looked up and said, "Listen. Can you hear boats?"

They listened and then ran across the island to look down the river. There were twenty or more boats on the water. Every boat in St. Petersburg was out.

"What are they doing?" asked Joe.

"They're looking for a dead body, I think," said Huck. "They did that last summer when Bill Turner fell in the river and drowned."

"Who's dead, do you think?" asked Joe.

The boys watched the boats. Suddenly, Tom cried, "I know who's dead! It's us! They're looking for us!"

This was wonderful. Tom looked at his friends. "We're famous!" he said. "Everybody in St. Petersburg is talking about us. And they all feel sorry for us!"

Night came, and the boys went to sleep. But Tom did not sleep, and when morning came, he wasn't there!

"Huck, where's Tom?" cried Joe.

"I don't know," Huck began, "but—look! There he is. He's swimming across to the island now. Hey, Tom!"

At breakfast Tom told his story. "I went home last night," he said, "and listened at the window. Joe, your mother was there, too, and she and Aunt Polly cried and cried. I heard some very interesting things. On Sunday there's going to be a big funeral at the church—for us! And listen—I have a wonderful idea."

Huck and Joe listened and laughed, and yes, it was a wonderful idea.

19

That night the boys cooked some more fish, and after dinner Huck got out his pipe and began to smoke.

"Can we smoke, too?" asked Tom. "I want to learn."

So Huck made pipes for Tom and Joe, and the three boys sat and smoked.

"Hey, I like smoking," said Tom. "It's easy!"

"It's nothing!" said Joe. "I'm going to smoke every day."

But after ten minutes Tom and Joe got quieter and quieter and their faces went an interesting color.

Tom and Joe got quieter and quieter.

"I'm going for a little walk now," said Tom. He stood up, carefully, and walked away into the trees.

"Me too," said Joe, quickly.

The two boys came back an hour later. But they didn't smoke their pipes again.

On Sunday morning there were no happy faces in St. Petersburg. Aunt Polly and Joe's mother and father were in the church, and all the boys' friends. The minister said some very nice things about the three boys, and the boys' families cried and cried. Everybody cried. And little Becky Thatcher did not stop crying for one second.

There was a small noise at the back of the church, but at first nobody heard it. Then the minister looked up—and suddenly stopped speaking. Everybody turned to look. Their mouths opened, and stayed open.

And into the church came the three dead boys—Tom first, Joe next, and then Huck.

And into the church came the three dead boys.

For a second nobody moved or spoke, and then the noise began. Aunt Polly and Joe's mother ran to the boys and took them in their arms. Aunt Polly cried, and laughed, and cried again.

"Oh, Tom!" she said. "You're a bad boy, but I love you!"

Suddenly, the minister called out, "Oh, happy days! Sing, good people of St. Petersburg! Sing and be happy!"

And everybody sang, and smiled, and laughed for a long time. It was St. Petersburg's happiest funeral.

The weeks went by, and the judge came to St. Petersburg. On the day before Muff Potter's trial, Huck and Tom met in the street near Tom's house. Huck was unhappy.

"Tom, you didn't tell anyone about—you know?"

"No, I didn't. But Huck, what about Muff? People are saying he's the killer. And he's going to die!"

"But we can't tell anyone about Injun Joe," said Huck. "I don't want to die, too! Do you?"

No, Tom didn't want to die. But he couldn't forget Muff Potter's face in the jail—old, tired, and unhappy. And Injun Joe was a free man. It wasn't right.

That night Tom came home late, and very excited. He could not sleep for two or three hours.

The next morning all the town was at Muff Potter's trial. Injun Joe was there, too. Muff waited, a tired old man with a dirty face. The judge began the trial.

Questions, questions, questions. Answers, answers, answers. And the answers were all bad for Muff Potter.

"Yes, I found the knife in the graveyard, next to Doctor Robinson's body."

"Yes, that's Muff Potter's knife. He always carries it."

"Yes, I saw Muff Potter in the town that afternoon. He had the knife with him then."

Questions, questions, questions …

23

Muff Potter began to look more and more unhappy. Then the judge said: "Call Thomas Sawyer!"

St. Petersburg sat up. What did young Tom Sawyer know? Everybody looked at him, and waited.

"Thomas Sawyer, where were you on the seventeenth of June, at the hour of midnight?"

"In the graveyard."

"Why?"

"I went there to see ghosts. With a—a—dead cat."

St. Petersburg laughed, and the judge looked angry. "And where were you in the graveyard, Thomas?"

"Behind the trees near Hoss Williams' grave."

Injun Joe's face suddenly went white.

"Now, my boy," said the judge. "Tell us your story."

And so Tom told his story, and St. Petersburg sat and listened to him with open mouths.

"... and then Muff Potter fell, and Injun Joe jumped with the knife and—"

Crash! Injun Joe jumped through the window, and was out and away in a second.

St. Petersburg loved Tom for a week. But Tom was not happy. Injun Joe was not in jail, and he was a dangerous man. Tom slept badly for weeks.

The slow summer days went by. Injun Joe did not come back to St. Petersburg, and Tom began to forget.

4

Treasure

There is a time in every boy's life when he wants to
and dig for treasure. And that time came for Tom.

So, one hot summer's day, he went to find Huck.

Huck liked the idea of treasure. "Where are we going
to dig?" he asked.

"An old dead tree is best."

"Who puts the treasure under old trees?"

"Robbers," said Tom. "And then they go away, or
they forget to come back for the treasure."

"There's a dead tree on Cardiff Hill," said Huck.
"Let's go there! I have an old pick and shovel."

It was three miles to the old tree, and the boys arrived
tired and hot. They dug for an hour or two, but they

"I have an old pick and shovel."

The boys watched through the holes in the floor.

didn't find any treasure. Then they stopped, and Tom looked down at an old house at the foot of the hill.

"Hey, look!" he said. "Nobody lives in that old house. Let's go there. Old houses are always good for treasure."

"Good for ghosts, too!" said Huck.

They took the pick and shovel with them, and went down the hill and into the old house. They looked in all the rooms downstairs, and then went upstairs. But there was no treasure, and no ghosts. Then they heard a noise.

"*Sh!*" said Tom, suddenly. "What's that?"

"*Ghosts!*" whispered Huck.

There were holes in the floor, and through them the boys could see into the rooms downstairs.

"No," Tom whispered. "It's two men. One is the old

26

Spaniard. He came to live in the town last week. I don't know the other man. Sh! Let's listen to them."

The two men sat down on the floor. The Spaniard had a green hat and long white hair; the other man was small and dark. He took out a bag and began to open it.

"It's hot in here," the Spaniard said. He took off his green hat—and then he took off his long white hair!

"*Tom!*" Huck whispered upstairs. "*That's Injun Joe!*"

"We took six hundred and fifty dollars when we robbed that house," said the second man. He took some money out of the bag. "We can take fifty dollars with us now. What are we going to do with the six hundred?"

"Leave it here," said Injun Joe. "We can come back and get it next week. Here, give me the bag."

He walked across the room to the fireplace, moved two big stones from the floor, and began to dig with his knife.

He began to dig with his knife.

Upstairs, the two boys watched excitedly. Treasure! Six hundred dollars of wonderful treasure!

Injun Joe stopped digging. "Hello, what's this?" he said. "There's something here. It's an old box."

The two men got the box out and opened it.

"It's money!" said Injun Joe's friend.

Injun Joe put his hand into the box. "There are thousands of dollars here!" he said, and the two men looked at the money with happy smiles.

"But who—" began Injun Joe's friend.

"Don't ask," Injun Joe said. "It's our money now."

"We can't take it with us today," said his friend. "What can we do with it? Put it back under the floor?"

"Yes," said Injun Joe. (Happy faces upstairs.) "No! (Very unhappy faces upstairs.) Let's put it under the cross—nobody goes there. We can take it there tonight."

When night came, the two men carried all the money away. The boys did not go after them because they were afraid of Injun Joe. But they wanted very much to find that "cross."

For a week the two boys thought and thought about the treasure. It was "under the cross," but where was the cross? In St. Petersburg the boys watched the "Spaniard" carefully, but they didn't see a cross, and they didn't find the treasure.

In the Cave

The next Saturday was Becky Thatcher's birthday, and all Becky's friends were very excited.

"It's going to be a wonderful day," Becky told Tom. "We're going to have a picnic by the river, and after that, we can visit McDougal's Cave."

So in the morning, a big boat took Becky, Tom, and all their friends down the river. There were some older children on the boat too, but all the mothers and fathers stayed at home. Picnics are better without them!

And it was a very happy, noisy picnic.

It was a very happy, noisy picnic.

For hours the children walked and ran through the cave.

After the picnic, the children took out their candles and ran up the hill to the cave. The mouth of the cave was dark, and some of the children were afraid at first. But caves are exciting, so in the end everybody went in.

McDougal's Cave was very, very big, with hundreds of tunnels and rooms. The tunnels went up, down, and into the hill for miles. You could walk for days in McDougal's Cave. Nobody knew all the cave, but many people knew the tunnels near the door. You could play all day in these tunnels. Tom, of course, knew them well.

For hours the children
walked and ran through the cave, up
and down the tunnels, in and out of the rooms.
In the evening they came out and walked down the hill
to the boat, tired but happy.

When the boat arrived back in St. Petersburg, it was
dark. Huck Finn saw the boat, but he did not know
about the picnic. He did not go to birthday picnics, of
course, because the mothers of St. Petersburg did not
like him. But tonight Huck was only interested in
treasure—Injun Joe's treasure. Injun Joe was in an old
building by the river, and Huck waited in the street near
the building.

"Perhaps," he thought, "Injun Joe's cross is in there,
and the box of money. I must wait and watch. I can tell
Tom about it tomorrow."

But Injun Joe didn't come out. At midnight it began to
rain, and Huck waited all night in the cold street. In the

morning he could not move and he could not speak. He felt cold, then hot, then cold, then hot again. Mrs. Douglas, a woman from the church, found him in the street. She took him to her home and put him to bed. And there he stayed for two weeks. He was very ill, and so he did not hear about Tom and Becky.

But on Sunday morning all St. Petersburg knew about Tom and Becky—because they were not on the boat when it came back to the town. Where were they? Were they lost in the cave? And were they alive or dead?

At first Tom and Becky played with their friends in the cave. Then Tom wanted to go down a new tunnel, and Becky went with him.

They walked, and talked, and went into a second tunnel, then a third. Sometimes Tom put a mark with

Sometimes Tom put a mark on the tunnel wall.

They ran into the nearest tunnel, with the bats behind them.

candle smoke on the tunnel wall—he wanted to find the mouth of the cave again! Then they came out of the tunnels into a big room. There were hundreds of bats in this room, and the candles woke them up. Tom took Becky's hand and they ran into the nearest tunnel, with the bats behind them. But one bat hit Becky's candle and it went out. The children ran and ran through the tunnels, and at last they got away from the bats. They stopped and sat down. Suddenly, it was very, very quiet.

"Where are we now, Tom?" Becky whispered, afraid.

"I don't know," said Tom. "I think it's time to go back. But we can't go through that big room because of the bats. Let's go down this tunnel."

They went down one tunnel, then a second, a third, a fourth ... Then they wanted to find the big room with the bats again, but they couldn't. Becky began to cry:

"Tom, we can't get out. We're lost, Tom, we're lost!"

They walked, and walked. When they were tired, they sat down. Then they got up and walked again. Time went by. Was it day or night? They didn't know.

Then Tom wanted to find water. They had nothing to eat, and they must have something to drink. They found a very small river and sat down next to it.

"Becky," said Tom. "We must stay here. Near this river. This is our last candle, and ..."

He did not finish, but Becky understood.

"Tom?"

"Yes, Becky."

"Are they going to come and look for us?"

"Of course! When the boat gets to St. Petersburg—"

"But how can they find us, in these *hundreds* of tunnels? Oh, Tom, Tom, we're going to die in here!"

Becky began to cry again. Then the candle went out, and the two children were in the dark. They sat for hours and hours. They slept a little, then woke up, and then slept again. Was it Sunday now? Or Monday?

Suddenly Tom sat up. "Listen! Somebody's calling!"

The two children listened. They heard it again, a little nearer. They called back; then they began to walk down the tunnel in the dark, with their hands on the wall. They stopped and listened again, but now they couldn't hear anything. Slowly, they went back to their river.

They slept again, and woke up very, very hungry.

"Perhaps it's Tuesday now," Tom thought. "What can I do? I must do *something*!" Then he had an idea.

"Becky, listen. I have a long string in my pocket. I can go down some of the small tunnels and get back to you with the string. You wait here."

Slowly and carefully, Tom went down the first tunnel on his hands and knees. Then the tunnel wall on his right finished, and there was nothing. Tom put out his hand to feel the floor. And just then, away to his right, he saw a hand—a hand with a candle.

Tom went down the first tunnel on his hands and knees.

35

At once Tom called out. "Help!" he cried.

The hand moved, and Tom saw an arm and a face. It was Injun Joe! Tom was very afraid, but Injun Joe was afraid too, and he quickly ran away down the tunnel.

Tom went back to Becky, but he did not tell her about Injun Joe. Tom waited for an hour, then went into a different tunnel with his string. Then a third tunnel ...

It was Tuesday evening, and St. Petersburg waited. Many of the townspeople were in the cave, and they looked for the children day and night. But they heard nothing, saw nothing, and found nothing.

Then, late that evening, there was a sudden noise in the streets. People began to run to the Thatchers' house.

"They're here! Becky and Tom are here!"

Most of the town came to listen to Tom's story.

"It was in the sixth tunnel," he told them. "I went to the end of my string, and suddenly, I could see daylight! There was a little hole in the cave wall. I put my head out, and there was the river, right under my nose! I went back and got Becky, and we climbed out through the hole. Then we stopped a boat on the river. We were five miles from the mouth of the cave!"

Tom was very tired after his three days in the cave, and he went to bed and stayed there for two days. He heard

"Suddenly, I could see daylight!" said Tom.

about Huck and went to see him on Sunday, and then every day. But Mrs. Douglas was always in the room.

"You can just say hello," she told Tom. "And then you must go. Huck is very ill, and he needs to sleep."

So Tom could not talk about anything exciting, and he could not tell Huck about Injun Joe.

One day, about two weeks after the picnic, Tom was in Becky's house, and her father came in.

"Well, Tom," Mr. Thatcher said. "Would you like to go back to the cave again, one day?"

"I'm not afraid of that cave," said Tom.

Mr. Thatcher laughed. "There are a lot of people like you, Tom. But nobody's going into the cave again. There are big doors across the cave mouth now—and nobody can open them!"

Tom's face went white. "But Mr. Thatcher—Injun Joe's in that cave!"

An hour later, fifty men were at the cave and they opened the doors. Injun Joe was on the ground, dead, his face to the door and his knife in his hand.

Injun Joe was on the ground, dead.

6

Under the Cross

The day after Injun Joe's funeral, Huck was out of bed. He and Tom walked slowly out of the town. They had a good, long talk, and Huck heard all about the picnic, the cave, and Injun Joe.

"We're never going to find the money now," said Huck.

"Huck," said Tom. "The money isn't in St. Petersburg. It's in the cave—I know it is! Why was Injun Joe in the cave? Because he took the box of money there! Right?"

Huck looked excited. "Say that again, Tom!"

"The money's in the cave! And we can get to it easily. Let's go there now! I have some candles and a long string. We can take a boat and put it back later."

Twenty minutes later the boys were in a boat on the Mississippi. They went eight miles down the river, and then Tom stopped by some small trees.

"Here we are!" he said.

Tom's hole was just behind the trees. Tom took a candle and climbed in. Huck climbed in after him.

"Injun Joe never found this hole," said Tom. "Or he did find it and couldn't get through it. It's very small."

The boys went carefully through the tunnels with their string. Then Tom stopped.

The boys went eight miles down the river.

"I saw Injun Joe about here," he said. "And look, Huck—there's the cross!"

There was a big smoke cross on the tunnel wall. The boys looked up and down the tunnel, but there was no box of money.

"Injun Joe said *under* the cross," said Tom. "Perhaps it's under the ground. Look, we can move these stones."

The boys took their knives and began to dig by the tunnel wall. Very soon, they found a second, smaller tunnel under the wall. They climbed down into it, and came into a small room. There was a bed, two whiskey bottles, some old shoes—and the box of money.

When somebody finds treasure, everybody hears about it very quickly. The two boys carried the box through the town. And when they got to Aunt Polly's house, half the town was with them. Everybody went into the house.

"Oh, Tom, Tom!" cried Aunt Polly. "What is it now? And what do you have there?"

Tom put the box on the table and opened it.

There were twelve thousand dollars in that box. And suddenly, Tom Sawyer and Huckleberry Finn were the richest people in St. Petersburg.

There were twelve thousand dollars in that box.

GLOSSARY

aunt   the sister of your mother or father
climb   to go up or down, using your hands and feet
cross   a mark like + or the letter X
cut   to make a hole in something with a knife
dangerous   something dangerous can hurt or kill you
drown   to die under water because you cannot breathe
empty   with nothing in it
funeral   the church service before you put a dead person into a
   grave
idea   when you think of something new, you have an idea (a
   picture or a plan) in your head
island   a piece of land with water around it
judge (*n*)   the most important person at a trial; he or she
   decides when somebody must go to prison
meow   to make a noise like a cat
rob   to take from a person or place something (money, gold,
   etc.) that is not yours
sheriff   the person in charge of the law and the police in a town
treasure   money, gold, silver, jewels, etc.
trial   the time when judges and other people decide who is, or is
   not, a robber, a murderer, etc.
unhappy   not happy
wake (past tense **woke**)   when you stop sleeping, you wake up
whiskey   a strong alcoholic drink
whisper (*v*)   to talk very quietly

The Adventures of Tom Sawyer

ACTIVITIES

Before Reading

1 **Read the back cover and the story introduction on the first page of the book. What does Tom Sawyer like?**
Check one box each time.

		YES	NO
1	school	☐	☐
2	swimming	☐	☐
3	getting up in the morning	☐	☐
4	work	☐	☐
5	fishing	☐	☐
6	adventures	☐	☐

2 **What is going to happen in the story? Can you guess?**
Check one box for each sentence.

		YES	NO
1	Tom and Huck see a ghost.	☐	☐
2	Tom and Huck find a lot of money.	☐	☐
3	Three men take some money from the graveyard.	☐	☐
4	Injun Joe kills someone.	☐	☐
5	Someone kills Injun Joe.	☐	☐

While Reading

Read Chapter 1. Are these sentences true (T) or false (F)? Rewrite the false ones with the correct information.

1 Tom lived with his mother and father.
2 Tom painted all the fence.
3 Huck Finn went to school.
4 Huck wanted to go and see ghosts.
5 Tom wanted to sit with the girls.
6 Becky Thatcher didn't like Tom's pictures.

Read Chapter 2. Who said this, and to whom?

1 "Oh, let's go home!"
2 "What are they doing here?"
3 "I gave you the money this morning."
4 "I want that money!"
5 "Don't hit my friend."
6 "Why did you kill him?"
7 "I'm afraid of Injun Joe."

Before you read Chapter 3, can you guess what happens? Choose one of these answers.

1 Tom doesn't tell the Sheriff the true story of the killing, and at the trial, they say that Muff Potter must die.
2 Tom tells the Sheriff the true story of the killing and Injun Joe goes to jail.
3 Tom tells the true story, but Injun Joe runs away.
4 Tom tells the true story and Injun Joe tries to kill him.

Read Chapter 3. Choose the best question-word for these questions, and then answer them.

Why / What / Where
1 ... couldn't Tom sleep?
2 ... was Jackson's Island?
3 ... did the boys have for breakfast?
4 ... did the boys see on the river in the afternoon?
5 ... happened to Tom and Joe when they smoked?
6 ... did the boys go on Sunday morning?

Read Chapter 4, and then answer these questions.

1 Why did Tom and Huck go to the old tree?
2 Where did they go after that?
3 How could they see into the rooms downstairs?
4 Who was the Spaniard?
5 How much money was in the bag?

6 What did Injun Joe find under the floor?

7 Where did Injun Joe want to put the money?

Read Chapter 5. Put these sentences in the correct order.

1 Tom saw Injun Joe, but Injun Joe ran away.

2 Soon, Tom and Becky were lost in the tunnels.

3 But then Tom and Becky left their friends.

4 One Saturday, a big boat took Becky, Tom, and their friends down the river.

5 Two weeks later, Mr. Thatcher told Tom that there were big doors across the cave mouth.

6 They needed water, so Tom found a small river.

7 So Tom and Becky got out of the cave and went home.

8 Fifty men went to the cave and found Injun Joe dead.

9 In the sixth tunnel, Tom saw daylight and found a hole.

10 All the children went into the cave.

11 Then Tom left Becky and went down a tunnel.

12 Tom and Becky went into a room of bats, and ran away.

Read Chapter 6. Here are some untrue sentences about it. Change them into true sentences.

1 Tom and Huck went into the cave through the doors.

2 They found a painted cross on the tunnel wall.

3 They found an empty box in the room at the end of the second tunnel.

4 Nobody in the town heard about the treasure.

After Reading

1 **What did Tom tell the judge at Muff Potter's trial? Match these halves of sentences to make his story.**

1 I went to the graveyard with a dead cat ...

2 Suddenly, I saw three ghosts, ...

3 Doctor Robinson was there with Injun Joe and Muff Potter, ...

4 They stopped at Hoss Williams' grave ...

5 Muff asked the doctor for five dollars more, ...

6 Then Injun Joe got angry with the doctor ...

7 Muff jumped on the doctor ...

8 The doctor hit Muff on the head ...

9 But Injun Joe had Muff's knife ...

10 and Muff fell down.

11 and the doctor hit him.

12 because I wanted to see ghosts.

13 and he killed the doctor with it.

14 but the doctor said "no."

15 and Joe and Muff started to dig.

16 but they weren't really ghosts. They were men.

17 and he and the doctor began to fight.

18 and I knew that they were grave robbers.

2 Here is a conversation between Aunt Polly and Tom. Complete Aunt Polly's questions. Use as many words as you like.

AUNT POLLY: Oh, Tom. You bad boy. I thought that you were dead. Where _____?

TOM: On Jackson's Island.

AUNT POLLY: Jackson's Island? Why _____?

TOM: Because we wanted to do something exciting.

AUNT POLLY: What's so exciting about Jackson's Island? There's nothing there. Where _____?

TOM: Under the trees. It was wonderful.

AUNT POLLY: Well, I don't know! What _____?

TOM: We took some bread and meat with us. Then, in the morning, we went fishing and got fish for our breakfast.

3 Here is a newspaper report about the treasure. Find the ten mistakes and correct them.

Two children, Tom Sawyer and Becky Thatcher, found twelve hundred dollars in a bag in McDougal's Cave. Muff Potter found the money under a tree and put it in a big room at the end of a tunnel. He marked the floor of the tunnel with a cross. But then he couldn't get out of the cave because of the ghosts at the mouth of the cave. When the men found him, he was alive, so there is going to be a trial.

4 Here is a new illustration for the story. Find the best place in the story to put the picture, and answer these questions.

The picture goes on page ____.

1 Who is telling his story to the judge?
2 Who is jumping through the window?
3 Why?

Now write a caption for the illustration.

Caption: _____

5 Imagine that you are lost in a cave. Which of these things are you going to use to help you? Make sentences like this.

You can use a/some _____ to _____.

bat, candle, knife, money, pipe, shoes, shovel, string, whiskey

6 Here are some new chapter titles. Match them with the chapter numbers. Do you like all of them? Why, or why not?

1, 2, 3, 4, 5, 6

Becky's Birthday Picnic	The Money in the Cave
Tom Paints a Fence	The Man with the Green Hat
Injun Joe Kills the Doctor	Tom and Becky Are Lost
Tom Smokes a Pipe	Ghosts
Tom and the Apples	The Old House
The Old Tree	Huck Gets Ill
The Happiest Funeral	A New Girl at School
Grave Robbers	Twelve Thousand Dollars
The Richest Boys in Town	Muff Potter's Trial

ABOUT THE AUTHOR

Mark Twain's real name was Samuel Clemens. He was born in Florida, a town in Missouri, in 1835 and he then lived in Hannibal, Missouri. When he was twelve, his father died, and he went out to work. He began to write for his brother's newspaper, and later he wrote for newspapers in Nevada and California. From 1857 to 1861, he was a river-pilot, guiding river boats on the great Mississippi river. The name "Mark Twain" came from his life on the Mississippi. The river-pilots called out words like these to the captain of the boat, and "mark twain" meant that there were two fathoms of water (about twelve feet) under the boat.

He started to write books of stories in 1867 and became famous for making people laugh. *The Adventures of Tom Sawyer* (1876) and *Huckleberry Finn* (1884) are his two most famous books. Many of the people and places in these stories are from the years when Mark Twain was a boy in Hannibal (Hannibal is the town of St. Petersburg in this story).

Mark Twain wrote many books. Some of them were important, some not so important, and he traveled to many English-speaking countries, talking about his work. Sadly, he had money problems, and his wife and two of his three daughters died before him, so his life was difficult and unhappy when he was older. He died in 1910.

OXFORD BOOKWORMS LIBRARY

Classics • Crime & Mystery • Factfiles • Fantasy & Horror
Human Interest • Playscripts • Thriller & Adventure
True Stories • World Stories

The OXFORD BOOKWORMS LIBRARY provides enjoyable reading in English, with a wide range of classic and modern fiction, non-fiction, and plays. It includes original and adapted texts in seven carefully graded language stages which take learners from beginner to advanced level.

All Stage 1 titles, as well as over eighty other titles from Starter to Stage 6, are available as audio recordings. All Starters and many titles at Stages 1 to 4 are specially recommended for younger learners. Every Bookworm is illustrated, and Starters and Factfiles have full-color illustrations.

The OXFORD BOOKWORMS LIBRARY also offers extensive support. Each book contains an introduction to the story, notes about the author, a glossary, and activities. Additional resources include tests and worksheets, as well as answers for these and for the activities in the books. There is advice on running a class library, using audio recordings, and the many ways of using Oxford Bookworms in reading programs. Resource materials are available on the website <www.oup.com/bookworms>.

The *Oxford Bookworms Collection* is a series for advanced learners. It consists of volumes of short stories by well-known authors, both classic and modern. Texts are not abridged or adapted in any way, but carefully selected to be accessible to the advanced student.

You can find details and a full list of titles in the *Oxford Bookworms Library Catalog* and *Oxford English Language Teaching Catalogs*, and on the website <www.oup.com/bookworms>.

The Elephant Man

TIM VICARY

He is not beautiful. His mother does not want him, and children run away from him. People laugh at him and call him "The Elephant Man."

Then someone speaks to him—and listens to him! At the age of 27, Joseph Merrick finds a friend for the first time in his life.

This is a true and tragic story. It is also a famous film.

Pocahontas

TIM VICARY

A beautiful young Indian girl and a brave Englishman. Black eyes and blue eyes. A friendly smile, a laugh, a look of love … But this is North America in 1607, and love is not easy. The girl is the daughter of King Powhatan, and the Englishman is a white man. And the Indians of Virginia do not want the white men in their beautiful country.

This is the famous story of Pocahontas and her love for the Englishman John Smith.

The Wizard of Oz

L. FRANK BAUM

Retold by Rosemary Border

Dorothy lives in Kansas, but one day a cyclone blows Dorothy and her house to a strange country called Oz. There, Dorothy makes friends with the Scarecrow, the Tin Man, and the Cowardly Lion.

But she wants to go home to Kansas. Only one person can help her, and that is the country's famous Wizard. So Dorothy and her friends take the yellow brick road to the Emerald City, to find the Wizard of Oz . . .

The Phantom of the Opera

JENNIFER BASSETT

It is 1880 in the Opera House in Paris. Everybody is talking about the Phantom of the Opera, the ghost that lives somewhere under the Opera House. The Phantom is a man in black clothes. He is a body without a head; he is a head without a body. He has a yellow face, he has no nose, and he has black holes for eyes. Everybody is afraid of the Phantom—the singers, the dancers, the directors, the stage workers . . .

But who has actually seen him?

Huckleberry Finn

MARK TWAIN

Retold by Diane Mowat

Who wants to live in a house, wear clean clothes, be good, and go to school every day? Not young Huckleberry Finn, that's for sure.

So Huck runs away and is soon floating down the great Mississippi River on a raft. With him is Jim, a black slave who is also running away. But life is not always easy for the two friends.

And there's 300 dollars waiting for anyone who catches poor Jim …

Dracula

BRAM STOKER

Retold by Diane Mowat

In the mountains of Transylvania there stands a castle. It is the home of Count Dracula—a dark, lonely place. At night the wolves howl around the walls …

In the year 1875 Jonathan Harker comes from England to do business with the Count. But Jonathan does not feel comfortable at Castle Dracula. Strange things happen at night, and very soon he begins to feel afraid. And he is right to be afraid because Count Dracula is one of the Un-Dead—a vampire that drinks the blood of living people …